LOVE, AN INDEX

Love, an Index

REBECCA LINDENBERG

MᶜSWEENEY'S
POETRY SERIES

MCSWEENEY'S

SAN FRANCISCO

www.mcsweeneys.net

Copyright © 2012 Rebecca Lindenberg.

Cover art by Brecht Evens.
This book was typeset in Fournier.

The McSweeney's Poetry Series is edited by
Dominic Luxford and Jesse Nathan.

McSweeney's and colophon are registered trademarks of McSweeney's,
a privately held company with wildy fluctuating resources.

Printed in Michigan by Thomson-Shore.

ISBN: 978-1-936365-79-1

for Craig Arnold
1967–2009

To the hands come
many things. In time of trouble

a wild exultation.

Robert Creeley

TABLE OF CONTENTS

WHAT RINGS BUT CAN'T BE ANSWERED

You are beautiful as a telephone, colors
of bone, rocket ship, and cocktail lounge—

Hmm, says the neon sign, starting
an unfinishable thought.

Where do we go from here?

I'm a balloon,
each minute you don't call is a breath
you blow into me.

I want to be the crackers in your soup,
I want to be your brass compass. Oh, mister,
just thinking about you curls the ends of my hair.

The clock *tisk-tisks*.

Moon, you old spinster, don't you mock me
with your pockmarks and your slow, slow travels.

Moon, what would you know, cold as cheese?

Hmm. Tisk-tisk.

Behind a far-off door, a thought about me is being formed
out of nothing but light.

And when that phone does ring—

GIRL WITH THE TYPEWRITER EYES

forms an ivory exclamation mark
in the black   circle

of her pupil   every time
he calls her
lovely.

In the other eye's dark key
appears a question mark—

she often wishes   her thoughts

were not so inscribed

in her expressions.

CARNIVAL

The mask that burns like a violin, the mask
that sings only dead languages, that loves
the destruction of being put on. The mask
that sighs like a woman even though
a woman wears it. The mask beaded with
freshwater pearls, with seeds. The plumed mask,
the mask with a sutured mouth, a moonface,
with a healed gash that means *harvest*. A glower
that hides *wanting*. A grotesque pucker. Here's
a beaked mask, a braided mask, here's a mask
without eyes, a mask that looks like a mask
but isn't—please don't try to unribbon it.
The mask that snows coins, the mask full of wasps.
Lace mask to net escaping thoughts. Pass me
the rouged mask, the one made of sheet music.
Or the jackal mask, the hide-bound mask
that renders lovers identical with night.

WHICH, IF I NEVER THOUGHT TO MENTION IT BEFORE, I NOW FEEL COMPELLED TO ADDRESS

Tall, tall, tall, tall, tall man

you bend so as not to dent the firmament.
You're made of elements I've never tasted.

I crave you, tall man,

I love your strident devotion to the real
as knowable.
I love your *bum-ba-da-bum*.
I love your thumbtacks and shrouds.

Wrap me in your arms and teach me
how to carol the moon
in a way that pleases it.

Yes, sometimes I want to pick up my shadow
and sling it at you—yes,
you make me so angry
I burst into green, green flames.

I love you. Forgive me,

I have made you the object
of poems, I have subjected you
to much wheezing.

Oh, tall man

love me like a hero
and I will give you an arrow from my quiver.
Bum-ba-da-bum.

Sublime. Sublime. Sublime.

Rome, 2005

LOVE, A FOOTNOTE

1. The KGB Bar off 2nd Avenue in New York's East Village was a gathering place for the Ukrainian Communist Party, which explains the curious décor but not the frequent readings.

2. Red is evoked by the longest wavelengths of light discernible to the human eye. Red is long; long and slow. The curtains in the KGB Bar are not so much red as a history of red.

3. "Podium," from the Latin, often confused with "lectern." One stands on a podium. One leans one's elbows or sets one's beer, beaded with condensation, on the lectern.

4. In ventriloquism, the speaker's voice seems to come from elsewhere. This doesn't explain why he called his poem "The Ventriloquist." Maybe something about the poet and the reader, but I don't like trickery, anyway.

5. We associate red with heat, energy, and blood, and with emotions associated with heat, energy, and blood—such as anger or love. Ezra Pound makes his ideogram of "red" with four signifiers: *rose, cherry, iron rust, flamingo*. I would use: *bark, blood, cardinal, sex*. Sex because, like red, it occurs in long, slow waves.

6. You sat next to me, though I didn't know you at the time. It was red, dark and red, and there was so much smoke you could see the air moving around people as they moved.

7. I love words that can inhabit more than one part of speech, as in *a* match or *to* match. The phosphorous smell of a just-lit match. Enough light for two faces to share.

8. Wallace Stegner's comment about art as the communication of insight appears in various incarnations in his work, but my favorite is in *Angle of Repose*. You acted surprised that I had such a thought. I took it as a compliment at the time.

9. In Plato's *Symposium*, Diotima tells Socrates how to experience the ideal form of beauty through love. From our desire to possess one body, we sense eternity.

10. An "angle of repose" is the slope at which granular materials come to rest at, say, the base of a sheer rock face. In Utah, owing to iron rust, the rocks are often red. The process is long, and slow.

11. As with "match," one can *be* patient, or one can be *a* patient. I have been both, but never at the same time.

12. Veselka is a Ukrainian diner in the East Village, near St. Mark's Church. Very good pierogi. Many of the customers have chic glasses, cases for musical instruments, and dirty hair. I like to sit at the counter.

13. Sake is produced by multiple fermentations of rice. Sometimes it tastes like heavy moonlight, sometimes it tastes like a neon sign that's just been turned off. In Japan, sake is drunk from small cups called *choku*. In certain friends' Lower East Side apartments in December, it is heated in a microwave and drunk from chipped coffee mugs that say things like "Happy Secretary's Day" and "#1 Dad," even though the person who lives there is neither a secretary nor a dad.

14. Feeling is a way of knowing what you're going to think about something. Example: I felt the thought, *I could want you*. Emotion as premonition. It is a mystery. It is the ideal form of beauty.

LITANY

O you gods, you long-limbed animals, you
astride the sea and you unhammocked
in the cypress grove and you with your hair
full of horses, please. My thoughts have turned
from the savor of plums to the merits
of pity—touch and interrupt me,
chasten me with awe. Seed god and husk god,
god of the open palm, you know the doubts
that harrow me, you know my wrists are small.
O you, with glass-colored wind at your call,
and you, whose voice is soft as a turned page,
whose voice returns the air to its forms, send me
a word for *faith* that also means *his thrum*,
his coax, and *her soft hollow*—please, friend gods,
so when he says, *You give it all away*,
                    I can say, *I am not sorry.*

FRAGMENT

bare knees   bare spine
bare
     windows

knuckles, your   chin
     cushion

flanks
        Yes   finger, lip

opening
       angelbones

poppyred
     birthmark

     your   if the

tattoos, words
       Soft
           words
    wrists
lungs   sternum

          bare stone

sunlight, sunlight   Limbs

ON THE SEA

Best of all things is water.
PINDAR

Hold a lamp over the edge of the pier, and the rays will come. Through the green halo, sea moths glide.

I have liked to lie in a room with doors open, to smell the tang of ocean fog.

My father's line went taut and the pole bowed deep. The boat lurched and water droplets spangled on the line like a strand of pearls. We watched an acid-green backfin carve a wake behind us, then disappear. My father cranked the reel until the dolphinfish bucked on the floor of the boat—then speared its throat. My mother watched the mood-ring fish fade from angry yellow-green back to the color of the sea in that place, and she cried for it.

Weave, weaver of the winds.

The fishwife's hands, old roots, unwind the woolen yarn. She cinches the sweater-knit taut as a stretched net. Later, they will know him by her patterns—lobster, rope stitch—and not by his angel-blue body, picked open by crabs.

Somewhere in the mist, a whale's stony back churns the surface.

A photograph: My sister and I, fingers stained blood-purple with the ink of a sea hare that refused to be dislodged from its home among the tide pools.

All the rivers run to the sea, and yet the sea is not full.

A photograph: Craig and I on a bench. Behind us, a harbor tessellated with hundreds of brilliant white sails.

CATALOGUE OF EPHEMERA

You give me flowers resembling Chinese lanterns.

You give me *hale*, for yellow. You give me *vex*.

You give me lemons softened in brine and you give me cuttlefish ink.
You give me all 463 stairs of Brunelleschi's dome.

You give me seduction and you let me give it back to you.
You give me *you*.

You give me an apartment full of morning smells—toasted bagel and black
coffee and the freckled lilies in the vase on the windowsill.
You give me 24-across.

You give me flowers resembling moths' wings.

You give me the first bird of morning alighting on a wire.
You give me the sidewalk café with plastic furniture and the boys
with their feet on the chairs.
You give me the swoop of homemade kites in the park on Sunday.
You give me afternoon-colored beer with lemons in it.

You give me D.H. Lawrence,
and he gives me pomegranates and sorb-apples.

You give me the loose tooth of California, the broken jaw of New York City.
You give me the blue sky of Wyoming, and the blue wind through it.

You give me an ancient city where the language is a secret
everyone is keeping.

You give me a t-shirt that says all you gave me was this t-shirt.
You give me pictures with yourself cut out.

You give me lime blossoms, but not for what they symbolize.

You give me *yes*. You give me *no*.

You give me midnight apples in a car with the windows down.
You give me the flashbulbs of an electrical storm.
You give me thunder and the suddenly green underbellies of clouds.

You give me the careening of trains.
You give me the scent of bruised mint.

You give me the smell of black hair, of blond hair.

You give me Apollo and Daphne, Pan and Syrinx.
You give me Echo.

You give me hyacinths and narcissus. You give me foxgloves
and soft fists of peony.

You give me the filthy carpet of an East Village apartment.
You give me seeming not to notice.

You give me an unfinished argument, begun on the Manhattan-bound F train.

You give me paintings of women with their eyes closed.
You give me grief, and how to grieve.

The Language of Flowers

Acacia: Secret Love
Asphodel: Regret
Bee Balm: Submission
Bindweed: Dashed Hope
Bird's Foot Trefoil: Revenge
Cabbage: Profit
Carnation (White): Disdain
Carnation (Striped): Refusal
Chrysanthemum (Yellow): Slighted Love
Dandelion: Coquetry
Eglantine: I Wound to Heal
Hollyhock: Ambition
Hypericum: Fidelity and Optimism
Lavender: Distrust
Lime Blossom: Fornication
Marigold: Grief
Mint: Suspicion
Plum: Lost in Beauty
Poppy (Red): Threatening Pleasure
Rose (Black): Transcending Love
Rose (Coral): Vicious Love
Rose (White): Hatred or Rebirth
Rose (Without Thorns): Youthful Love
Sage: I Will Not Survive You

The Language of Flowers, *Revised*

Bird of Paradise: Good Intentions

Cactus: Second Chances

Crocus: Commitment Phobia

Eucalyptus: O God What Have I Done

Hops: Chemistry

Jasmine: Allure

Juniper: Kindness

Lamb's Ear: You've Changed Me

Lotus: Consolation

Mandrake: Going Off Birth Control

Millet: Hospitality

Mimosa: Gratefulness

Mullein: Refuge

Nasturtium: Vigor

Nettle: Candor

Orchid: Vulnerability

Phlox (Sweet William): Levity

Poppy (California): Nostalgia

Rose (Dried): Fantasy

Rose (Glass): Narcissism

Rose (Paper): Affection

Rose (Red): Hysterical Longing

Rose (Sand or Desert): Resentment

Rose (Tin Foil): Rejecting Another's Advances

Saffron: Hollowed by Absence

Venus Flytrap: Sexual Bliss

Vine (Ivy): Codependency

Wheat: I Took Nothing for Granted

TUMULT

I'd wake with you

next to me brooding—   you said your heart
was a trapdoor

      we kept falling through.   Once
I was so angry
     I threw my shoes at you—

my faults   so petty, now
     technicolor,   numerous—

this tendency to reduce you and me   to story—

a late-night airport pick-up   the long drive
     home through a blizzard
(galaxy of snow-stars   all in hyperdrive)

following the plow
     down a closed highway
  talking
about the Romantics
     their thoughts on revolution

while your son read *Harry Potter*   under my coat;

dinner on a rooftop
     the elevated train

jangling the marquee,
      a cinematic backdrop;
                we were falling
through the same sky
      though you broke
down doors in our home.   You held

your bald head in your hand   saying

      you were a puppet
          on the strings of your own appetites

dancing
      observing the dance   unable to stop

being   in your body
         its heart-engine

      shuddering and stalling and

asking things of your hands   you would

      call them back from
         if you could.
This boundless need of yours

for wonder—
      how demanding you could be
of what I have

      and do not have   to give.

GREEK EASTER

Bury me, your son
demands. Warm sand

leaves black dust
on our palms. We heap

his goosepimpled legs,
damp swimsuit,

soft belly, crossed arms.
He laughs, wiggles

his toes out and we
bury them again. *No,*

he says, *bury me*
all the way. So we place

a towel over his face,
blanket it with grit.

We can see sand rustle
when he breathes.

Do you want to come out?
we ask. *Nmph*, he muffles.

Perissa (Thira), 2006

An Appetite for Rain

The rain in L'Aquila battered the pavement
in whatever Italian is for *battered*

the pavement. Some grace note
slur of consonants—*sfu* or *gli*—

that means the sound of rain
ruining itself upon the ground.

We went to the fortress to see the art
guarded therein, but I let myself be

distracted by the luminous emerald
grass around the fortress, your son

hurling pinecones into the moat.
We watched the sky descend and said

we would remember this. Side-by-side
we stood in the perpetual green.

L'Aquila, 2006

ILLUMINATING

you said when you were a kid, you'd say to yourself: I will remember this. and then you would remember it, whatever it was, in every detail

I would have said *bikes* or *motorcycles* but the sleeveless drunk gentleman at the diner was good enough to give us a brief tutorial in biker gang slang and custom

I do not believe I remember any of this wrong, but there is a reason I have left bits out

you also said something about the olden days, sending youths out into those bleak hills with a bow and single arrow (here you motion shooting yourself with it) in case they couldn't handle it—it being some kind of quest, but you didn't specify

memory is just perception unless you commit the sin of seeing it in some other way

We press the heels of our palms into the soft gray rock of the Dakota Badlands, leaving a print for the wind and rain to erode. I haven't yet realized that I left my wallet in the gas station bathroom about a hundred miles back. Instead I'm laughing at your remark that a certain lonesome patch of grass in the midst of this landscape would make a perfect croquet pitch. From time to time a gang of hogs roars by on its way to the rally at Sturgis. The sky is blues and yellows, and the air is damp with cold. The car is warm, but its window is cold against my bare forearm, resting on the passenger's side door. When, at the visitor's center I realize my wallet is gone, I call the gas station and the friendly attendant takes my address to mail it home to me. You say, *What would you want your wallet for anyway?*

When we get to the Black Hills, the gold is pink and sold in every diner, truck stop, and tourist jeweler from Mount Rushmore to Spearfish. We try to see the Crazyhorse Monument, but it isn't finished yet. After driving all over because you just have to find the perfect buffalo burger, we end up back in Wyoming, at Devils Tower. You're harassing the prairie dogs, shouting into one of their tunnels, *Bald Eagle! Bald Eagle! Come in! This is Jumping Frog at Checkpoint Charlie! Hole number 37 has been compromised! Repeat! Hole number 37 has been compromised! I'm reading the sign that says to avoid the prairie dogs because they can carry bubonic plague. I say, Hey, Jumping Frog, I think you should back away from Hole 37.* All this in the shadow of a massive trunk of basalt, its perfectly hexagonal granite columns ascending skyward into the Western sun.

known in Medieval Europe as Black Death; the Middle Ages, sometimes called Dark, were in fact a time of great transformation, whose texts we call "illuminated"

at times I want to ask you if you remember this the same way but when I try to imagine what you'd say I find it's like trying to play both sides of a chessboard

the old wooden rungs of a ladder wedged between stone columns remain here but should not be climbed—they are barely driftwood, and the top of Devils Tower teems with venomous snakes, escapees from nesting hawks, prisoners of the pitch where no snake belongs and so the more vicious

than it was given to you at the time. do not be seduced by those who would call that "learning," they are the same fools who peddle guilt, and when has guilt kept any of the promises it made to its followers?

if you can recall how it felt at the time you can grasp that the end changes nothing

those illuminated manuscripts were mostly copied by illiterate scribes who traced the shapes of the letters, leaving two columns around the text—one for the errata of the master scribe, who proofread their work, the other for the scholia or interpretive commentary of the reader. The effect is a kind of textual lucidity, a conversation, which none may resolve but any might partake of

Versus

Man vs. Bird

The man envies the bird.
The bird will never fall in love
and say *I can't.*

The bird flutters
in circles over its nest,
startles at the rustle of leaves.

The man, who can't inhabit
the anxious mind of a bird, thinks

I wish I could fly.

Bird vs. Snow

The bird knows *snow*
has no opposite.

Nor does *sea*, nor *machine*,
nor *despair*.

The bird doesn't know
it's the only creature possessed
of this knowledge,

so it doesn't try to tell
the man, the woman,

the bright unbroken sky.

Bird vs. Lamppost

The lamppost dims,
the sky flaps like a sheet.

Shadows hurry back
into their objects.

A moth—
tattered and damp
hem of a dress—
shivers on the glass.

The bird takes the moth.

It will eat the small body,
quilt its nest with the wings.

Woman vs. Snow

The woman in the snow

 carves wide
wings around herself.

The bird swoops low.

Man vs. Woman

The woman lies on her back
as women sometimes do.

The man tries to speak to the bird
in its language
but the bird hears

a slight human accent
and takes to the branches.

The woman imagines herself falling
into the sky

while the man falls slowly
into himself,

quiet and wanting and afraid.

Woman vs. Herself

Her skin is cold
and damp as a window.

She looks at herself in the glass
and thinks *Yes*

I have that to give.

Sun diminishes
frost on the pane.

Outside, the sound of ice.

They are   your heart stutters to see
the letters of another alphabet
a vast lace of calligraphy
a hundred thousand characters of praise.

CRAIG ARNOLD, "Mistral"

Love, an Index

A

ABANDON, what I did when you touched me
    that winter with an ungloved hand.
ACHE, broken things healing: bones, disappointments.
ALLEGORIES
    of Love, Fragonard's gossamered paintings,
        Ovid's pursuers and storied looms. The longing
        to know how things become what they weren't always.
    of Death, the *danse macabre* on a grave
        with a skull-faced man. What should knowing we'll die elicit?
        What does salvation have to do with being safe?
ANGELBONES, *scapular acromia*. Where the wings
    uncouple. Where the wings belong.
APARTMENTS,
    Brooklyn, its spiral staircase reminding me
        of Francis Bacon: "All men rise to greatness by
        a winding stair." A bicycle chained there.
    South Dakota, we gave your son the only bedroom, woke early
        to salted baguette and snow.
    Salt Lake City, a porch ghost, a view
        of the valley's glittering grid, my sister, your
        poor broken friend; we grilled
        squid on the Smokey Joe.
    Laramie, a basement, a stoveless kitchen,
        toaster-roasted eggplant, baseboard
        heat and sex in woolen socks.
    Rome, 5B, stone floors, kitchen
        white as the madness I felt there, a bed made

from twin beds held together with duct tape,
always suggesting itself as metaphor.

ANGER,
yours, with your father, maybe
with me.
mine, with you for expressing it
toward my family; there are other ways
of telling the story of our two angers, entwined
like bodies in the act of love. But in this one
I am not a villain.

ANNE CARSON,
the "Short Talks" from *Plainwater*, poolside
in Greece while an Easter Parade clanked
pots and pans, congregating in doorways
for ouzo and bread;
Autobiography of Red, in which Geryon
understands that people need
acts of attention from each other.

ANTELOPE ISLAND, you should have seen my father's face
as the herd of bison loped across the road,
not ten feet from where we sat in our rented car.
We watched the grace pool out around their
hooves. I suppose you cannot make statements
about the loveliness of something
until you have watched it move.

ATTENTION (See also: ANNE CARSON)
"[Geryon] understood that people need acts of attention from
one another."

B

BABETTE, the cat. You were angry when I got her
   because I hadn't consulted you. And what,
   I asked, do you ever consult me about?
   I got to keep the cat. She slept on your chest,
   you were such a still sleeper.
BINARY,
   code, allows a computer to represent text—b
   is "01100010." L-o-v-e is a series
   of 1s and 0s where 0 means "off" and 1 means "on."
   opposition, such as presence / absence, sex / innocence, desire /
   attainment, form / rapture, you / I.
   star, two astronomical bodies orbiting each other
   so closely their lights knit and appear as one.
BOGOTÁ, city in the Andes surrounded by steep
   jungle. We did not fight in Bogotá.
   The Mexican restaurant full of wooden stairs
   overlooks expanses of Modernist architecture,
   colonial plazas, lit-up slums. La Candelaria,
   home to statues of ghosts, presence of absence.
   Vendors sell hot corn. We passed a woman
   laying on the sidewalk, her pregnant belly
   swollen in half-globes around a dark scar
   like a peach around its deep groove. Storytellers
   ride the buses, scattered petals and piles of thorns
   and broad bruised leaves carpet the lot
   of a flower market that teems by day. Sushi joint.
   Iranian embassy. Buildings trimmed
   with tropical flowers and razor wire. We watched
   Bollywood dubbed into Spanish on the dial-tune TV
   in your sublet apartment.

BOLLYWOOD, where love is an exuberant fantasy
of song, where a story stops before it ends.

C

CALIFORNIA, where I lived and where you lived,
    as it turns out, at the same time. You were
    just graduated from Yale, working at a theater and
    I was in the fifth grade. You had a roommate
    whose salads were legend and a girlfriend
    whose father taught you to cook *bún thit nuóng*.
    I had a bicycle with a banana seat and my sister and I
    used it to play Tollbooth in the carport, or ride
    to the pool, stopping first at the store for French bread
    and ranch dressing or burritos for a snack.
CALIFORNIA, a few years later
    I went to that theater—my friend was house-sitting
    in the Haight. We made daiquiris in the fancy blender,
    smoked Nat Sherman mint cigarettes on the porch,
    watched the city lights spangle and thought, *We are so cool.*
CHOPIN,
    étude. Major keys seem to have
        to do with light, minor keys
        with shadows cast by major keys.
    nocturne, an evocation of watchful owls,
        satin, violins. Or a woman
        at a desk trying to see through
        her own reflection in the window.
    prelude, a text that is all preface, forward
        to a story untold.
COMFORT,
    erotic. As in Campion: "when we come
        where comfort is, she never will say no."
    food. For me, thick sourdough toast,
        the pickled herring of childhood Christmases.

For you, peanut butter on black German bread
or a carefully peeled grapefruit. Your son craves
red curry spicy enough to make both your noses run.

COMPROMISE, I will get up early with you
so long as you've made coffee.

CONVERSATION
about poems, you like "the sound of rice
poured into a pan." I like "the bird
who sings like a wetted wine-glass rim,"
and "the bird who casts its shadow on the sea." I like
poems held between two people "Lucky Pierre style."
(See also: PERSONISM.) With Coleridge, "And when I rose
I found myself in prayer." Such poems gather
everything into the *now* of the poem. I want
to gather everything into this poem's *now*,
but can't. All is gloss (See also: GLOSS).

COQUETTE, you called me once. Coy, you said. I am
neither. I am all candor and anxiety.
Even those words embarrass me.

D

DEADWOOD, ringing with slot machines. We drank pear wine
in a stale motel. I said "you take me
to awll the noicest places." You funny-voiced
me back, "Whaddya want? They got ice machines,
they got HBO, dial up some va-va-voom." We showered
together and your peppermint soap gave me chills.
DESIRE, a chord played deep in the bass of the body
loud enough to drown yourself out.
DIDO, Queen of Carthage. A mighty widow, rebuilder
of ruined empires, devotee of the gods.
Ruined by rumor, by love, ruined unto death
by a traveler who was nobody's king.
DIVORCE, far from a way you thought you had
of thinking of yourself. This story
includes a divorce, which is how I come in.
D.H. LAWRENCE (See also: DESIRE) tells us "no, no, it is
the three strange angels. Admit them, admit them."

E

EMILY, my sister, when asked what single thing
    she'd bring to a desert island, said, "a yacht."
    Like me, she fears to make mistakes.
EPITHET,
  Homeric, such as "swift-footed," even when the hero's sitting down,
    or "breaker-of-horses." For women, "soft-braided"
    or "glancing." I have some for you, tall man.
    You have some for me.
EROS, son of Aphrodite, who according to Seneca
    "smites maids' breasts with unknown heat
    and bids the very gods leave heaven
    and dwell on earth in borrowed forms."
EX-, a prefix meaning "formerly and no more,"
    connoting renunciation when affixed
    to nouns such as "lover" and "Catholic";
    not likely to be placed before certain other
    nouns, such as "sister" or "bicycle."
EYE, in the Middle Ages it was thought impossible to desire anything
    you've never seen, and so the blind could not love.
EYE, lens and retina, vitreous humor,
    ocular nerve and filigree of capillary veins. For years
    my blood sugar has been gathering like rust
    in these tiny pipes. They clog or weaken, crack,
    leak. Black smokes in my eye.

F

FATE, about which Breton and Éluard asked in an issue of *Minotaure:*
    "What was the most significant moment
    of your life, and did you recognize it at the time?"
    Sunflower. Clocktower. Love revealed,
    unpursued. Umbrella. Sandwich. Despite ourselves.
FIAT,
    Panda, we drove from the church to the party, five of us
    smooshed in the tiny car—Kathryn in the back
    between Robin and Geoff. After the wedding,
    we drove south to the only town in Ireland
    ever ransacked by pirates. As you and I finished
    some wine in the courtyard, a badger
    came snuffling out of the lush undergrowth
    looking for scraps. "Sit up on the table," you said,
    helping me. "Wild creatures can be unpredictable."
    "Okay," I hiccupped, lifting my feet.
    Ulysse, we took to Sulmona to visit Ovid's birthplace, to walk
    cobbled streets strung with Christmas lights, to buy the little
    foil-wrapped candy almonds they call *confetti*, gathered
    into grape-clusters, daisies, pussywillows, candy corsages.
    On the way to the Parco Nazionale, rain and hairpin
    mountain curves sent a sedan fishtailing into us. The *carabinieri*
    wanted to know if there were bears
    in our part of America. Yes, we said,
    many bears. Man-eating bears? Yes, of course,
    many man-eating bears.
FIRE, you and your son were always setting things ablaze—
    firecrackers, pinecones, tissues to watch them burn
    to ash before they touched the floor.

FORBIDDEN

> fruit, such as pomegranates or hidden flesh.

> love, one of my least favorite euphemisms. I might understand
>> forbidding sex-to-feel-powerful or sex-to-feel-charitable
>> or sex-to-feel-visible, but love? That, I cannot understand.

FORGIVE, we did. A lot.

FRAGMENT, I am a fragment of us. I am a fragment composed
> of fragments. Mosaic, pastiche, ruin. Everyday
> consciousness proposes lightbulb, ropeswing, teapot,
> David Bowie, your sweater on, your sweater off, tomatillo,
> all associated. Parts suggesting the whole
> they long to be gathered into.

G

GLOSS, a word is not an epitaph but it is not the thing
    it signifies, either. Except perhaps: the Word,
    which may be why it was there in the beginning
    and was God.

GREECE, in Delphi there's a mountain
    fringed with red poppies where we saw
    a goat herder listening to his iPod and to his goats,
    their spangled bells.

GUILT, not a feeling but a way of perceiving
    the fact that I didn't tell you to stay in Yakushima
    or go straight to Okinawa, skip the side trip. If you can't
    stop seeing this way, you become the king
    who had to put out his eyes.

GUITAR, covered in bumper stickers such as "I Heart
    Mormon Pussy" and "Dip Me In Honey &
    Throw Me to the Lesbians" and "Jerry Falwell
    Can Suck My Tinky-Winky" and on which
    you played "Hallelujah" with your eyes closed.

H

HACIENDA GUACHIPELIN, a farm in Costa Rica near Rincón de la Vieja
    on the Nicaraguan border. You climbed a volcano while I
    rode a horse with a *vaquero* named Henry. Waterfall,
    coatimundi. I met three stewardesses at a hot spring
    who painted me with mud, curing my sunburn. Gin and tonics
    by the pool. You kept rolling your glass across your brow.
    A woman carrying a sloth up the mountain asked,
    "Do you want to touch my sloth?" You said no,
    pretty sure she'd try to charge you.
HARBINGER, a sign, a messenger, an omen that precedes change.
    One night in April, I dreamed you coming to me.
    When I woke, the phone was ringing. The man
    on the other line said, "I have to talk to you.
    It's about Craig."
HEART, José Asunción Silva put on a white shirt
    and went to the doctor. He asked the doctor to draw on his shirt
    the exact size and location of the human heart in the body.
    Silva went home, loaded a pistol, muzzled it dead center
    of the outline, and fired.

I

IDEALIZE, to abstract oneself. A handsome woman
      is not "Home"; a lightning-struck tree is not
      "Judgment"; a handful of tea is not "Bitter Harvest."
IDOLIZE, to make of an idea a thing, to object-
      ify. In this way, an idea of harvest is found
      in a stone woman with stone breasts.
INTERSTATE, 80, one stretch of which traverses
      Utah and Wyoming. Sometimes we drove it,
      stopping at Little America for almond M&Ms,
      Diet Coke, and gas. Sometimes we were driven
      like snow, or in a bus with itinerant preachers,
      bleary young mothers, deadheading truckers,
      gangsters, and vampires. One guy with a get-out-
      of-Dodge ticket from the Reno police—
      I bought him a coffee because he looked so sad.

J

Julian of Norwich says "sin is behoovely," meaning
    "fitting," meaning only by sinning can we
    receive God's mercy. Good, I sin a lot.
    She also says, "All shall be well, and all
    shall be well, and all manner of thing shall be well."
Just, not in the sense of "right" or "fair" but "simply" or
    "enough." Example: Just because the world is beautiful
    doesn't mean it will satisfy us.

K

KUCHINO-ERABU-SHIMA, an island (See also: VOLCANOES). You called me
    from the ferry. I was talking about Zukofsky,
    you were saying you hated Zukofsky. You were happy and told me
    I would hate it there, the sea was very rough. You said
    "I love you, I miss you." I said, "I love you, I miss you, too."
    You said, "Tell Robin I love him."
    That's as far as I went with you.

L

LARAMIE, Wyoming, a university town with ceaseless wind.
    I brought my cat, read Sappho at the coffee shop
    near the rail line. Every now and then we'd walk
    to the Buckhorn for a beer and I would say
    something about the two-headed calf
    mounted on the wall and the bullet holes
    in the mirror, and you would say,
    "You always say something about those."
LEMON,
    Meyer, you brined them for tagine. How I love that word, *tagine.*
    soap, when I got out of the shower you grinned,
    "You're a clean little lemon drop. C'mere."
LOVE, what we call it when it keeps feeling that way.
    But what is *it*? A private language? A motion
    ever towards? A memory the body keeps
    of those palms on my flank? And must it
    be a kind of mourning? (See also: ATTENTION,
    COMFORT, DIDO, HEART, JUST, X.)
LYRIC, a quiet mode of minor praise
    or meditation. When the epic is over
    and all the heroes are dead and the wanderers
    have come home and the enslaved women
    have learned the language of their new land, lyric
    will pour the wine, tune the instruments, sing
    of cold hearth fires, the brambles and vines
    retaking the forsaken city.

M

MAD LOVE, Breton's book for his daughter
    about his love affair with her mother, in which he writes:
    "What I have loved, whether
    I have kept it or not, I shall love forever."
MIMOSA
    cocktail, tangerine juice and sidewalk
        traffic and smoke-colored clouds and your tomato-
        colored sweater and my tomato-colored
        lipstick left all around the rim
        of the tall glass this lazy city Sunday birthday morning.
    flowers, yellow tufts wafting around Venice,
        in the hands and behind the ears
        of mothers and girlfriends, wives
        or men on their way to visit sisters
        and lovers on Festa della Donna, this day
        when, with a handful of frail gold blossoms
        men give thanks for their women.
MYTH, a narrative that tells the origin of something,
        something's transformation into
        a new form. Narcissus becomes a blossom,
        Io becomes a white calf and then
        herself again. (See also: ANGELBONES, DIDO,
        EPITHET, FRAGMENT, QUANDARY, SACRIFICE.)

N

NEVER, writing it again and again, I become
     estranged from it. *Never never never never never.*
NEW
   Haven, where we ate pizza with eggplant on it, walked
      in the shadows of dark stone buildings, a ritual
      you used to perform with someone else.
   York, where we met and kept coming back to sleep
      on air mattresses and eat lasagna and soup dumplings,
      drink wine at the little French place
      where I used to work. "My little street urchin,"
      you called me then, sipping espresso at the bar.

O

O, a gesture for invoking a spirit or god
      in supplication, for example. *O, Pallas! O, Kypris!*
      My mother's maiden name, like
      Aphrodite's alias, means "from Cyprus."
OH, a sound suggesting startlement, appropriate
      to situations of spiritual amazement and erotic bliss,
      but also polite boredom or the horror of learning
      the person who really knew you has died.
OMAHA, where we'd go to the Antiquarium for old books,
      the Zen Center for poetry slams, and to that one
      Persian restaurant, the chicken stewed in pomegranate-
      walnut sauce, conjuring what it might be like
      to sleep under a heavy rug in a desert palace in wintertime.
OVER, when I answered the phone
      that May morning and the man from the search team
      said, "It's over."
OVER, as in turn over, start over, get over. To get
      to the other side of the same story.

P

PARTNER, this feeble word we use to introduce each other:
    "This is my partner Craig," and "This is Rebecca,
    my partner." What word explains how, with you,
    everything meant something—a drive through Abiquiu
    with *A Passage to India* playing on tape; a Scrabble argument
    after which you touched my face and said, "Fair enough";
    sharing a bottle of wine that tasted like fresh Band-Aids
    while we boiled the carcass of a chicken for stock
    so I could show you how to make risotto. And what
    is the word for me now? (See also: WIDOW.)
PERSEPHONE, the maiden, Queen of the Dead.
    You wrote her a hymn about "the grace
    to release our beloveds kindly into her care."
    I am trying.
PERSONISM, I cannot pick up the telephone
    and call you, so I write you poems.
PIZZA
    al taglio, cut with scissors, priced by weight, sold by the bus stop
        or beside the bridge; porcini mushrooms, rosemary and *lardo*, *bianca*
        with olive oil and sea salt, sleeved in grease-flimsy paper.
    al fondo, its own plate, *mozzerella di bufala* just sour, soft,
        a dense cumulus weeping onto red basil.
POETRY, how thought feels.
PSYCHE, the nymph who gives us psychic, psychology,
    psychopath. Eros was her lover, so long
    as they met only in darkness. Curious, she lit a lamp—
    we still think of love as irreconcilable
    with intellect. She's depicted with butterfly wings
    and it was thought that when you die, your soul flutters
    as a moth from your open throat.

Q

QUANDARY, a problem with no solution. (See also: DESIRE.)

R

RE: Bug's School Conference, Re: guest list, Re: Of course,
   Re: no way, Re: OMMFG, Re: poems, Re: more poems,
   Re: when you get a chance, Re: Mexico, Re: asshole student
   behavior advice, Re: beautiful, Re: Oh, Reginald,
   I'm so bored I do wish the London season would begin,
   Re: Yes!, Re: Yay!, Re: Amazing, Re: don't hate me,
   Re: And that's what I mean when I talk about gods.
RISK, "What you risk reveals what you value," Winterson
   writes. "You play, you win, you play, you lose. You play."
ROME, shopping for vegetables. You held my hand as we wandered
   the Esquiline market, where an Arab vendor
   told us we could see his fish were freshest because
   their eyes most resembled glass. The rabbits all have
   ears so customers can be sure they aren't stray cats.
   We stopped at the gyro place, bags bristling with onion stems
   and fennel. Back home we left our bags slumped
   in the kitchen and lay down together in our bedroom,
   high ceilings salt-white in the profusion of afternoon
   sun. I remember my eyes stung with the excess of light.

S

SACRIFICE, you always said, "It's not a zero-sum game"
    and I always said, "It all evens out in the end."
    I still believe both are true, and
    that we have not yet come to the end.
SALT, when the Romans sacked Carthage, so the story goes,
    they sowed the earth with salt. Ezra Pound says
    "It is difficult to write a paradiso
    when all the superficial indications are
    that you ought to write an apocalypse."
SANCTIFY, "When the sun rises," Blake writes, "do you not see
    a round disc of fire somewhat like a guinea? O no, no, I see
    an innumerable company of the heavenly host crying Holy, Holy,
    Holy is the Lord God Almighty."
SAPPHO wrote lyric poetry of which mostly fragments
    remain. Only her "Hymn to Aphrodite" is whole. It ends
    "Come to me now: loose me from hard / care
    and all my heart longs / to accomplish,
    accomplish. You / be my ally."
SENTIMENTAL, I don't know what this word means. Sometimes
    it means maudlin, sometimes kitsch. What is the opposite
    of sentimentality? Is it restraint? Is it silence?
SISTINE CHAPEL, where I took my mother her first day in Rome.
    We stopped looking when my mother's eyes were full.
    "I studied this," she said. "I never imagined
    I would get to see it." That was my best day.
SKYPE, you turned your screen
    to face the hostel wall and said, "Okay, go"
    and I lifted my shirt.
SPLIT, Croatia, after Diocletian died, the local Dalmations, tired
    of being pillaged, took refuge in his deserted palace

and began to build. Here and there, the city's floor has collapsed
into the building's basement, a dank underworld
of illegal olive oil stills and bomb shelters, hideouts for petty thieves.
Makeshift gangplanks bridge these holes that collect
soccer balls, old bicycle tires, punk rock graffiti.
There's a street named "Let-Me-Pass," a harbor
full of Saudi Arabian yachts and Swiss schooners,
a promenade lined with smoking teenagers. I'd once loved
a man from there. You sent me with an archeological expedition
to do my own digging. Something in me, under
all those layers of now-being-loved, still felt left.

T

Tear Gas, Labor Day in Colombia, parades
        of people dressed all in yellow. We took the funicular
        up to Monserrate and you caught the little boy
        trying to pick your pocket. You just teased him.
        We walked down the winding path they said
        teemed with bandits. No bandits.
        On our way to visit the man who sells emeralds
        we found ourselves in an alley blocked by riot police.
        We turned down another street and I said
        "What's that smell? It's like air freshener—"
        "We have to go," you said. "This way. Right now."
Telephone
    bill, all those phone calls to Bogotá. I can see
        you sitting in the *abuelita*'s apartment, feet on
        the desk, leaning back in your chair and miles away
        me on my side across a made bed, listening
        to you talk about the performance artist
        who spent all day handing out leaflets downtown.
        It took seven months to pay it off.
    mobile, for so long you refused to have one. It had been,
        you said, the downfall of your first marriage.
        But I had to have one, you insisted.
        It wasn't safe otherwise. This meant you could always
        find me, but not the other way around.
Torrey, Utah, near Capitol Reef. We went to see the petroglyphs,
        pioneer graffiti in the slot canyons. In summer
        we picked enormous cherries in the public orchards
        sizzling with bees. There were always smashed apricots
        in the sun-stricken dirt. Plastic bags bulging with fruit.

We stopped at Café Diablo for crispy duck,
salad slippery with wild mushrooms. I miss that.
TRANQUILITY, another thing you gave me that I didn't have before,
and I am losing it again.

U

ULULATE, to keen, to wail in lamentation. There have always been
cultures that paid women to mourn, to join together
to make a voice big enough for that much feeling.
UN-, a prefix indicating negation, a way of giving
and taking away, the presence of absence: un-
loved, unbuttoned, ungrateful, un-lost. When asked
what one thing God could not do, Medieval
theologians said: Un-create.
US, our friend drew us each a picture—in yours, you're naked,
howling into a microphone, cock flouncing front-stage.
In mine, I am walking with a sack over my shoulder,
bent under a burden of leaves.

V

VANISH, dematerialize. *Poof!* How does one sail
    to the land of vanished things? And what color
    does your flag have to be to get back?
VOLCANOES, we visited many: Vesuvius looming over Naples
    like a history of violence and Pompeii's ash
    packed around a man-shaped hollow. The perfect cone
    of Stromboli. Cloud-forests sweating around Poás,
    its caldera cupping an aquamarine lake of boiling acid.
    Thira's thin crescent rising from the sea. A Mexican church
    half-submerged in basalt. A cobbled path of fractured granite
    descending into the North Atlantic. I thought I understood
    your longing—it looked so much like mine.
VOLKSWAGON,

  Golf (green), from Salt Lake City to Omaha in a day.
    You were so angry because I'd stayed up late
    the night before and couldn't drive the first shift.
    Later that summer, Duluth, Sault Sainte Marie,
    Montreal, Marblehead. *Harry Potter* on tape,
    your son asleep in the back with his feet on my lap
    and his head resting on your guitar.
  Golf (red), I could see you coming from so far
    down the snowed-in road. Me at the bus station
    freezing my ass off. You cranked the heat,
    plucked off my wool cap, put your mouth over my ear.
VOW, I think as much now about the ones we failed to make
    as the ones we faithfully kept.

W

WIDOW, a woman whose husband has died.
    So, not me. But many of the obelisks
    in the Provincetown cemetery commemorate
    captains and whalers lost at sea and their widows.
    In this sense, I am like those women.
WITTGENSTEIN says, "The world is all
    that is the case." Once I wrote it: "The word
    is all that is the case." (Also: "Pubic parks." Oh well.)
WORDS, I love, for instance, "radio," "milk,"
    "diaphanous," and "smudge." This has to do
    with their sound, ways they mean, and how they look
    unsurrounded on a page or written in marker
    across the back of a hand, as you used to do
    when you didn't want to forget.
WRITE, a grocery list or a name and telephone number
    on the title page of a book or corner of a coaster.
    Write emails requesting voter registration forms, write out
    prescriptions. Write your name on a marriage license
    or a birth certificate or bond. Write a love letter.
    Write a play about a man who looks at things
    and is made better by them, who looks
    at things that make him sad. Write a statement of purpose.
    Here is my statement of purpose: Yes, you.

X

X, marks the spot. Sex, vex.
      Hex. (See also: Ex-)
XXX, the lit-up symbol in a smutty magazine shop,
      parking lot crammed with eighteen-wheelers
      and one lonely BMW sedan.
        "Ever been to one of those?" I asked you.
        "No," you said, "You can't learn anything
        about sex from porn."

Y

YES, *yes I said yes I will Yes.*

YOU (See also: ACHE, BINARY, COMFORT, EROS, FATE,
FORGIVE, LOVE, *MAD LOVE*, MYTH, O, OH, PARTNER,
RISK, TELEPHONE, WRITE, XXX, ZENITH.)

Z

Zenith, the peak, the perfect.
Zephyr, the other wind. Not the mistral
    but the green-faced wind
    with its cheeks puffed out. The stir
    of tablecloths, sundresses, curls.
    The messenger of spring.

[   ]

CIRCUS ANIMAL

My mind is a tough sinew.

You can be so hard.

This sackcloth heart
holds a mad animal.

Hush, spleeny goblin.

We will rig up a house-machine

with paperclips and lipstick, oven-mitts
and lengths of garden hose.

We'll gild it to distraction.

You can be so hard.

I wish I didn't have to be

a box that fastens, I wish
for a gentle robber
who can pick locks with his tongue.

Hush, hush, heart-monster—

I'm varnishing
the bone-ladder.

Don't worry, he'll be back

any minute now.

OBSESSIONAL

I'm tired of getting over things.
MARTHA RONK

What makes a man impossible to find
on such a chip of land it's hardly there?
Could it be worse than what I have in mind?

I know where you are not, but I'm still blind
to any trace of *how* or *when* or *where*—
what makes a man impossible to find?

I wonder, is this ignorance more kind
than knowing what transpired? Does this spare
my wits from worse than what I have in mind?

I feel sometimes as though this world's designed
to show me how *without you* can't compare
to *with you*, man impossible to find.

I still can't pack away things that remind
me how you'd put your mouth around my ear
and breathe into me what you had in mind.

Someday I hope I can become resigned
to knowing it's *not knowing* I must bear.
What makes a man impossible to find?
Could it be worse than what I have in mind?

LOSING LANGUAGE: A PHRASEBOOK

He lived a good life: *I envied him a little.*

My condolences: *You look like you've been trying to drown yourself.*

My sympathies: *I fear to say something that might make it worse.*

Life goes on: *Don't forget us just because we're still alive.*

He was doing what he loved: *There is still such a thing as a good death.*

He'll always be with you: *You don't have to try so hard.*

You're so brave: *I wonder what it's like when you're alone.*

You're so strong: *I can see you've showered.*

You've handled it with such grace: *You've done nothing that can't be repaired.*

Let me know if you need anything: *I won't come around again.*

He lived so much in one lifetime: *He did just as he pleased.*

He lived large: *I saw him drunk. He laughed with his mouth wide open.*

He lived well: *He knew things, how the soul is electrified running your thumb across a lover's bottom lip, how a good martini makes a breeze inside the skull.*

He was a wonderful father: *Whatever else I may have thought of him.*

He was so loved: *His exes seem unusually distraught.*

He loved you so much: *What was private is now a secret.*

Time heals all wounds: *Including the ones he gave you before he died.*

I am very sorry for your loss:	*I am very sorry for your loss.*
I am very sorry for your loss:	*You are very sorry for my loss. You may not understand it. But then, I do not understand it.*
It takes time:	*You changed to belong with him. You learned, for instance, that he made excellent poached eggs and liked driving long distances. Now you must re-learn to spoon in just enough vinegar, and how not to be hypnotized by the fleeting white dashed lines.*
It's not right:	*How is this grimacing salesman in the world and not he?*
It's just terrible:	*If I could, I would give the gods this salesman in exchange—I would, without hesitation, to have my lover back.*
We can't know the reason:	*It's just as well the gods do not approach me with an explanation. Or a deal.*
One day perhaps, we'll understand:	*It is true, I am less afraid to die now.*
Thank you:	*For the casserole, the box of wine, for the walk—I needed to feel the sun on my hands.*
Thank you:	*For cleaning the cat box, for watching me nap. For the money.*

Thank you: *When I didn't know where to put my*
                                    attention, for your conversation,
                                    thank you.
Thank you: *For not leaving me alone.*

The Girl with the Ink-Stained Teeth

knows she's famous
    in a tiny, tragic way.
        She's not

daft,   after all.

She's been drinking
fountain
    pen ink,   hoping

it won't look like   suicide.

At the drunken party
    she announced

if she was gonna off herself
    she'd stage something

    madcap   enough
to compare
        to the tall man
who vanished, leaving her

nothing   not even
    her name.

The Girl with the Microfilm Face

wakes,
makes coffee,   takes showers
in slow motion

even crossing the street
looks like moiling   up steep hills

See the stories scroll
as she recites, again

interviews: the last thing
he said to her, why

he was knocking around
volcanoes   anyway,

evidence   he wouldn't
intentionally vanish

Headlines: SEARCH TEAMS!

Then, obituaries.

She gets back in the shower, slowly
tries again

to get the newsprint   off her skin
not realizing

it's a projection: all she has to do
is stand in the light.

GHOSTOLOGY

The whistler's
inhale,

the white space
between *is*

and *not*
or after a question,

a pause. Nothing
isn't song:

a leaf hatching
from its green shell,

frost whorling
across a windshield,

an open door
opening.

LOVE, N[1].

1. *an unnamable ideal; a desire created by the idea of that desire; a perfectly understood absence, not unlike the uncanny contours of Pompeii's small craters—ash packed around a man-shaped hollow; a hole, and what it holds*

C 600 BCE *Sappho* (fr. 105a) As a sweet apple turns RED on a high branch,/ high on the highest branch and the applepickers forgot—/ well, no, they didn't forget—were unable to reach   1855 *Robert Browning* ("Two in the Campagna") Just when I seemed about to learn!/ Where is the thread now?/ Off again!/ The old trick! Only I discern—/ INFINITE passion and the pain/ Of finite hearts that yearn.   1962 *Robert Duncan* ("A Poem Beginning with a Line by Pindar") GOD-STEP at the margins of thought   1962 *Robert Creeley* ("For Love") Yesterday I wanted to/ speak of it, that SENSE above/ the others to me/ important because all/ that I know derives/ from what it teaches me.

2. *erotic splendor*

C 60 BCE *Catullus* (*Plyometrics*, 5) Give me a thousand kisses, then a hundred,/ another thousand next, another hundred,/ a thousand without pause & then a hundred—/ then when we have notched up all those thousands,/ shuffle the figures, hiding count of the total/ from ourselves & any who would harm us,/ envying the wealth of OUR TRADE IN KISSES.   1633 *John Donne* ("Elegy 19, To His Mistress Going to Bed") Full nakedness! All joys are due to thee;/ As souls unbodied, bodies unclothed must be,/ To taste WHOLE JOYS [...] Then, since that I may know,/ As liberally as to a Midwife show/ Thyself: cast all, yea, this white linen hence,/ There is no penance due to innocence   c 1863 *Emily Dickinson* (J 1247, "To pile like thunder to its close") For none SEE GOD and live.   1964 *Denise*

Levertov ("Song for Ishtar") In the black of desire/ we rock and grunt, grunt and/ SHINE   1987 *Jeanette Winterson* (*The Passion*) I say I'm in love with her, what does that mean? It means I review my future and my past in the light of this feeling. It is as though I wrote in a foreign language that I am suddenly able to read. Wordlessly she explains me to myself; like GENIUS she is ignorant of what she does.   2005 *Craig Arnold, drowsing in afternoon sun on a bed in Rome, occasionally calling back to birds he doesn't recognize* I am FULL out to the skin   2008 *Craig Arnold* ("A Place of First Permission") As when you put yourself within a kiss/ so perfectly you lose all definition/ beyond mouth and fingers moving/ patient and presently and OPEN/ and you are full out to the skin.

3.   *one who loves; one who is beloved; one who comes to the apartment with fist-fuls of Thai basil and thin chilis and one who lets him feed her broth that hits high notes in the throat; one who has a poppycolored birthmark beneath his eye and one who looks for it*

C I BCE *Ovid* (*Ars Amatoria*) Wine makes all men/ Lovers. C 1120 *Guilhem IX, Duc d'Aquitaine* ("Song 1") Some people go vainly boasting of love;/ WE have the morsel and the knife.   1347 *Francesco Petrarca* (*Il Canzoniere*, 61) Blessed was the day, the month, the year/ and the season, the time and hour and moment/ and the beautiful country, the place where togeth-er/ two fine eyes found and BOUND me fast.   1595 *Edmund Spenser* (*Amoret-ti*, 75) My verse your virtues rare shall eternize,/ and in the heavens WRYTE your glorious name./ Where whenas death shall all the world subdew/ Our love shall live and later life renew   1807 *Samuel Taylor Coleridge* ("Recol-lections of Love") YOU stood before me like a thought,/ A dream remem-bered in a dream.   1957 *Frank O'Hara* ("Meditations in an Emergency") I am the least difficult of men. All I want is BOUNDLESS love.   1667 *John Mil-ton* (*Paradise Lost*, XII.648-649) They, HAND IN HAND, with wandering steps and slow,/ Through Eden took their SOLITARY WAY.

4. *the opposite of war and therefore inescapably political; provenance of private, individual triumph or lamentation rather than a subject (i.e., valor in battle) for public or civic joy; a distraction or diversion from duty and so a threat to imperialism; often characterized as feminine; subject of lyric in opposition to traditional epic values*

C 600 BCE *Sappho* (fr. 16) Some men say an army on horseback and some say an army on foot/ and some men say an army of ships is the most beautiful thing/ on the black earth. But I say it is/ WHAT YOU LOVE.   19 BCE *Virgil, trans. John Dryden* (*Aeneid*, Book 4) But good Aeneas, tho' he much desir'd/ To give that pity which her grief requir'd;/ Tho' much he MOURN'D, and labor'd with his love,/ Resolv'd at length, obeys the will of Jove;   1623 *William Shakespeare* (*Antony & Cleopatra*, I.i) The triple pillar of the world TRANSFORMED/ Into a strumpet's fool.   1909 *F.T. Marinetti* ("The Founding and Manifesto of Futurism") We will glorify war—the world's only hygiene—militarism, patriotism, the destructive gesture of freedom-bringers, BEAUTIFUL IDEAS WORTH DYING FOR, and scorn for woman.   1960 *Frank O'Hara* ("Having a Coke With You") and the fact that you MOVE so beautifully more or less takes care of Futurism.

5. *a Jacob's ladder, a staircase to the infinite; a means to an end wherein the end might also be the means*

380 BCE *Plato* (*The Symposium*) This is the RIGHT method of approaching love […] Like someone using a staircase, he should go from one to two to all beautiful bodies, and from beautiful bodies to beautiful practices, and from practices to beautiful forms of learning […] what beauty really is.   426 *St. Augustine* (*De Doctrina Cristiana*) This is the important difference between temporal things and ETERNAL things: something temporal is loved more before it is possessed, but will lose its appeal when attained […] The

eternal, on the other hand, is loved more passionately when attained than when desired.   2002 *Jessica Piazza recounting a conversation with her Aunt Helen, on a stoop in Brooklyn* Now, goils, of cawse you have to marry feh love. But remembah: It's jahst as easy to love a RICH man as it is to love a poah man.

6. *where the real finds its apogee; truth or at least honesty in the form of fearful nakedness, of candor; the mundane everyday constellation of facts that make up a relationship; the self we fear that somebody might see; the self we can only see reflected in somebody else's gaze*

C 30 BCE *Propertius* (I.ii. "Natural Beauty") Why choose, my life, to step out with styled hair/ And move sheer curves in Coan costume? [...] Love, BEING NAKED, does not love beauticians.   1633 *George Herbert* ("Jordan I") Who sayes that fictions only and false hair/ Become a verse? Is there no TRUTH in beauty?   1917 *Gertrude Stein* ("Sacred Emily") Rose IS a rose is a rose is a rose.   1997 *Olena Kalytiak Davis* ("A Few Words for the Visitor in the Parlor") Every time you wish the sky was something HAPPENING to your heart, you lose twice.   2004 *Craig Arnold to his partner, who was having difficulty choosing a dress for a party, having chosen to wear an orange dress instead of a gold dress, having chosen to wear lipstick but no other "warpaint," as he always called it, having come into the living room where he was sipping a martini* You're so pretty, YOU could be a spy.   2005 *Richard Siken* ("Litany in Which Certain Things Are Crossed Out") Okay, so I'm THE DRAGON. Big deal./ You still get to be the hero.

7. *that which indescribable grief is evidence of; the wound and its balm*

C 965 BCE *?King Solomon* (Song of Songs) I will SEEK him whom my soul loveth; I sought him, but I found him not.   1557 *Francesco Petrarca trans.*

Sir Thomas Wyatt (*Il Canzoniere*, 134) I FIND no peace, and all my war is done;/ I fear and hope; I burn and freeze like ice;/ I fly above the wind, yet can I not arise;/ And nought I have, and all the world I seize on [...] Likewise displeaseth me both death and life;/ And my delight is causer of this strife.   1609 *William Shakespeare* (Sonnet 116) Love's not TIME's FOOL, though rosy lips and cheeks/ within his bending sickle's compass come,/ Love alters not with his brief hours and weeks,/ but bears it out even to the edge of doom.   1789 *William Blake* ("The Clod and the Pebble") Love seeketh not Itself to please,/ Nor for itself hath any care,/ But for another gives its EASE,/ And builds a Heaven in Hell's despair.   1802 *William Wordsworth* ("Intimations of Immortality") THOUGH nothing can bring back the hour/ Of splendour in the grass, of glory in the flower;/ We will grieve not, rather find/ Strength in what remains behind   1917 *D.H. Lawrence* ("Bei Hennef") STRANGE, how we suffer in spite of this!   1962 *Robert Creeley* ("Kore") O love/ where are you/ leading/ me NOW?

MAD SONG

Fear not fair weather, my lord
as storm's herald.

For you, a lily
obscene-scented.
For you, a little night lunacy.

I am queen! Everything
I touch turns to sand.

Here is a beggar on a bridge, filling an hourglass
with a lover, a trinket, a thought
I almost got into words—

he will sell it for a ducat.

Poppies, bring poppies!

I float in the bathtub
so I must be beautiful.

Anger hollows the bones.

Throw in the acacia blossoms!

Good grief, sweet ladies, good grief,
sweet ladies. Good grief.

In the Museum of Lost Objects

What thou lov'st well shall not be reft from thee;
What thou lov'st well is thy true heritage.
    Ezra Pound

You'll find labels describing what is gone:
an empress's bones, a stolen painting

of a man in a feathered helmet
holding a flag-draped spear.

A vellum gospel, hidden somewhere long ago
forgotten, would have sat on that pedestal;

this glass cabinet could have kept the first
salts carried back from the Levant.

To help us comprehend the magnitude
of absence, huge rooms

lie empty of their wonders—the Colossus,
Babylon's Hanging Gardens and

in this gallery, empty shelves enough to hold
all the scrolls of Alexandria.

My love, I've petitioned the curator
who has acquired an empty chest

representing all the poems you will
now never write. It will be kept with others

in the poet's gallery. Next door,
a vacant room echoes with the spill

of jewels buried by a pirate who died
before disclosing their whereabouts.

I hope you don't mind, but I have kept
a few of your pieces

for my private collection. I think
you know the ones I mean.

STILL LIFE
WITH MOVEMENT

Fruit ripens in
the argent bowl.
The pear's slow
blush comes
as the burnished
salmon spoils,
woolly eyes forget-
ful. The rabbit's
trapped soul swells,
fur amplified
in the convex
silver dish. On this
cedar table all
the quiet volition
of the world underway,
becoming, then
becoming anew.

Status Update

Rebecca Lindenberg is drinking whiskey. Feels guilty. Is caught in one of those feedback loops. Is a blankity-blank. Is a trollop, a floozy, a brazen hussy. Would like to add you as a friend. Would like to add you as an informant. Would like to add you as her dark marauder, as her Lord and Savior. Has trouble with boundaries. Rebecca Lindenberg is keeping lonesomeness at bay with frequent status updates designed to elicit a thumbs-up icon from you. Rebecca Lindenberg likes this, dismisses this with a backhanded wave. Rebecca Lindenberg wraps her legs around this. Has a ball of string you can follow out of her labyrinth. Has this labyrinth. Rebecca Lindenberg has high hopes. Has high blood sugars. Rebecca Lindenberg doesn't want to upset you. Wants to say what you want to hear. Rebecca Lindenberg thinks of poetry as the practice of overhearing yourself. Rebecca Lindenberg thinks about love. About ribbons unspooling. Rebecca Lindenberg would like to add you as a profound influence. Would like to add you as a loyal assassin. Would like to add you as her date to the reckoning. Rebecca Lindenberg remembers a statue of a faceless girl with shapely feet. Rebecca Lindenberg remembers the Italian for "chicken breasts" is *petti di pollo* and the word for kilogram is *kilo* and that a kilo is way too much chicken breast for a family of three. Steals sage from strangers' gardens. Runs for it. Misses Rome. Misses her family of three. Is lost in her own poem. Rebecca Lindenberg has dreams in which you come back. Rebecca Lindenberg lets it go. Rebecca Lindenberg crescendos and descrescendos. Rebecca Lindenberg is: *Hey, you, c'mere.* Rebecca Lindenberg is: *You are not the boss of me.* Rebecca Lindenberg is not the boss of you. Rebecca Lindenberg goes to movies. Needs a bigger boat. Gave you her heart and you gave her a pen. Can't handle the truth. Rebecca Lindenberg loves the truth. Loves the smell of dirt gathered in water and the sleep-smell of your morning body. Loves her rumpled cat, her jimmied window. Loves long letters. Will write soon.

FRAGMENT

How you always

    those soft hands of

head on my belly

    I asked what you were thinking, you laughed,
said "Something about yellow curry." I laughed and

    listen, it's just

(Not that you'd mind.)

AUBADE

I woke in a gold dress,
you, in jeans.

Morning filled
wine bottles in the kitchen.

Fine mica glitter
of fish scales and salt.

Outside, it was quiet.

You said: *That went well,
don't you think?*

Sun behind you

I kissed the hole in the light
and said: *Yes.*

Status Update (2)

Rebecca Lindenberg is in a relationship and it's complicated. Rebecca Lindenberg is single and it's complicated. Rebecca Lindenberg joined the group "It All Seems So Simple Now, In The Aftermath Of This Consciousness-Altering Tragedy." Rebecca Lindenberg desires to keep desiring. Rebecca Lindenberg seizes the day, wants to go to bird-watching in Nicaragua. Wants to walk the Lake District. Rebecca Lindenberg wonders at the lavender sky over these red rocks. Wonders at the silvery smell that precedes lightning, and where these owls live in this expanse. Rebecca Lindenberg is Eden-bound. Rebecca Lindenberg has the audacity. Rebecca Lindenberg joined the group "I Wish I Looked Like A Piece Of Birthday Cake." Rebecca Lindenberg joined the group "Play With Me, Play With Me!" Rebecca Lindenberg will be the French waitress if you'll be the movie star. Will be the bandit if you'll drive the get-away car. Rebecca Lindenberg became a fan of "Talking About Sex Makes Us Blush." Rebecca Lindenberg became a fan of "Blushing."

Dispatches from an Unfinished World

A leaf the green that a child would choose
if asked
to draw a leaf.

*

This heavy-petalled rose
is humid as the accent
of my current correspondent.

*

Trees unberried by bird.
Trees unleafed by beetle.

*

My correspondent
is a tentative man and I
am unaccustomed to tentative men.

*

White rose blossom
browning at the edges.
Paperback book.

*

Inside, my mother humming
a song I've never heard.

*

Kinds of holiness.

*

Trees unbarked by winter deer.

*

My correspondent
will not let me love him.

*

Green things make
such mild noise.

*

I uncross my legs
to find, with a bare foot,
that sun has warmed the stone.
I partake of the sun.

*

And the stone.

MARBLEHEAD

not to be in love with you
I can't remember what it was like
it must've been lousy
JAMES SCHUYLER

You take off your black
motorcycle jacket, hang it
on the back of a chair. It's cold
from our walk along the sea wall.
Your pockets jingle with shells.
While we were gone, you left
the stove on low—some things
you do make me so nervous.
You graze the surface of sauce
simmering in a pan, shiny fingertip
held out for me to lick, you say
"What does it need?" Maybe nothing,
maybe honey to unbitter the lime.
Later that night you'll bury your face
in my belly and sob. "I'm sorry,"
though I don't think you are
always talking to me, my love.
But now lobster steam billows
up the window, you gulp
purple wine, your pinky sticking out,
and the round olives are the green
all green things aspire to be.

ACKNOWLEDGMENTS

Many thanks to the editors of the following publications in which these poems first appeared, sometimes under other titles and in earlier versions: *32 Poems*, the *Believer*, *Blaze Vox*, *Colorado Review*, *Conjunctions*, *Connotation Press*, *DIAGRAM*, *Gulf Coast*, *Mid-American Review*, *No Tell Motel*, *The Offending Adam*, *Poetry*, and *Pool*.

Thanks also to the National Endowment for the Arts, the Provincetown Fine Arts Work Center, and the University of Utah for generous fellowships that supported the completion of this project.

NOTES

The following texts and authors are either directly quoted or deliberately and substantially paraphrased as follows:

LOVE, A FOOTNOTE

Plato (trans. Christopher Gill). *The Symposium*. New York: Penguin Classics, 2003.

Pound, Ezra. *ABC of Reading*. New Haven: Yale University Press, 1934.

Stegner, Wallace. *Angle of Repose*. New York: Penguin Books, 2000.

ON THE SEA

1 Eccl. 7, *The Holy Bible: King James Version*. Nashville: Thomas Nelson Publishers, 1984.

Joyce, James. *Ulysses*. New York: Vintage Books, 1990.

Pindar, trans. Richard Lattimore. "Olympia I". *The Odes of Pindar*. Chicago: The University of Chicago Press, 1947.

CATALOGUE OF EPHEMERA

Lawrence, D.H. "Bei Hennef". *The Collected Poems of D.H. Lawrence*, ed. Vivian de Sola Pinto, Warren F. Roberts. New York: Penguin Books, 1994.

Lawrence, D.H. *Birds, Beasts and Flowers*. Charleston, SC: Nabu Press, 2010.

Spicer, Jack. "Five Words For Joe Dunn on His 22nd Birthday". *The Postmoderns: The New American Poetry Revised*, ed. Donald Allen. New York: Grove Press, 1994.

LOVE, AN INDEX

Andreas Cappellanus. *The Art of Courtly Love*. New York: Columbia University Press, 1990.

Blake, William. "A Vision of the Last Judgment". *Blake's Poetry and Designs (NCE)*, ed. John E. Grant and Mary Lynn Johnson. New York: W.W. Norton & Co., 2007.

Breton, Andre (trans. Mary Ann Caws) *Mad Love*. Lincoln, NE: University of Nebraska Press/Bison Books, 1988.

Campion, Thomas. "I care not for these ladies". *The Norton Anthology of English Literature Volume 1*, ed. Stephen Greenblatt et al. New York: W.W. Norton & Co., 2006.

Carson, Anne. "Short Talks". *Plainwater: Essays and Poetry*. New York: Vintage Books, 2000.

Carson, Anne. *The Autobiography of Red*. New York: Vingate Books, 1999.

Coleridge, Samuel Taylor. "The Nightengale: A Conversation Poem". *The Complete Poems of Samuel Taylor Coleridge*, ed. William Keach. New York: Penguin Classics, 1997.

Heidegger, Martin. "Language". *The Norton Anthology of Literary Theory and Criticism*, ed. Vincent Leitch et al. New York: W.W. Norton & Co., 2001.

Joyce, James. *Ulysses*. New York: Vintage Books, 1990.

Julian of Norwich. *The Showings of Julian of Norwich (NCE)*, ed. Denise N. Baker. New York: W.W. Norton & Co., 2004.

Lawrence, D.H. "Song of a Man Who Has Come Through". *The Collected Poems of D.H. Lawrence*, ed. Vivian de Sola Pinto, Warren F. Roberts. New York: Penguin Books, 1994.

O'Hara, Frank. "Personism". *Selected Poems*, ed. Mark Ford. New York: Knopf, 2008.

Sappho (trans. Anne Carson), *If Not, Winter*. New York: Knopf (Virago), 2003.

Winterson, Jeanette. *The Passion*. New York: Grove Press, 1997.

Wittgenstein, Ludwig. "Tractatus Logico-Philosophicus". *The Wittgenstein Reader*, ed. Anthony Kenny. Malden, MA: Blackwell Publishing, 1994.

Obsessional

Ronk, Martha. "I sat at the window and watched it cover everything by nightfall". *Vertigo*. Minneapolis, MN: Coffeehouse Press, 2007.

Love, n[1].

Song of Solomon, *The Holy Bible: King James Version*. Nashville, TN: Thomas Nelson Publishers, 1984.

Arnold, Craig. "A Place of First Permission". *Made Flesh*. Port Townsend, WA: Copper Canyon Press, 2008.

Blake, William. *Blake's Poetry and Designs (NCE)*, ed. John E. Grant and Mary Lynn Johnson. New York: W.W. Norton & Co., 2007.

Browning, Robert. *Robert Browning's Poetry (NCE)*, ed. James F. Loucks and Andrew M. Stauffer. New York: W.W. Norton & Co., 2007.

Catullus (trans. Peter Green). *The Poems of Catullus: A Bilingual Edition*. Berkeley: University of California Press, 2007.

Coleridge, Samuel Taylor. *Coleridge: Poetical Works*, ed. E.H. Coleridge. Oxford: Oxford University Press, 1969.

Creeley, Robert. *Selected Poems 1945-2005*, ed. Benjamin Friedlander. Berkeley, CA: University of California Press, 2008.

Davis, Olena Kalytiak. *And Her Soul Out Of Nothing*. Madison, WI: University of Wisconsin Press, 1997.

Dickinson, Emily. *The Complete Poems of Emily Dickinson*, ed. Thomas H. Johnson. New York: Little Brown/Back Bay Books, 1976.

Donne, John. *John Donne's Poetry (NCE)*, ed. Donald R. Dickson. New York: W.W. Norton & Co., 2007.

Duncan, Robert. *Selected Poems*, ed. Robert J. Bertholf. New York: New Directions, 1997.

Guilhem IX (trans. Bond, Gerald A.) The Poetry of William VII, Count of Poitier, IX Duke of Aquitaine New York: Garland Publishing Co., 1982.

Herbert, George. *The Metaphysical Poets*, ed. Helen Gardner. New York: Penguin Classics, 1960.

Lawrence, D.H. *The Collected Poems of D.H. Lawrence*, ed. Vivian de Sola Pinto, Warren F. Roberts. New York: Penguin Books, 1994.

Levertov, Denise. *Selected Poems*, ed. Paul Lacey. New York: New Directions, 2003.

Marinetti, F.T. (trans. Doug Thompson). *Critical Writings: New Edition*, ed. Gunter Berghaus. New York: Farrar, Strauss & Giroux, 2008.

Milton, John. *Paradise Lost (NCE)*, ed. Scott Elledge. New York: W.W. Norton & Co., 1992.

O'Hara, Frank. Selected Poems, ed. Mark Ford. New York: Knopf, 2008.

Ovid (trans. Allen Mandelbaum.) *The Metamorphoses*. New York: Mariner Books/Houghton Mifflin Harcourt, 1995.

Petrarch (trans. Sir Thomas Wyatt). *The Norton Anthology of English Literature Volume 1*, ed. Stephen Greenblatt et al. New York: W.W. Norton & Co., 2006.

Petrarch (trans. David Young). *The Poetry of Petrarch*. New York: Farrar, Strausse & Giroux, 2005.

Plato (trans. Christopher Gill). *The Symposium*. New York: Penguin Classics, 2003.

Propertius (trans. Guy Lee). *The Poems*. New York: Oxford University Press, 2009.

Sappho (trans. Anne Carson). *If Not, Winter*. New York: Vintage Books, 2003.

Seneca (trans. John Fitch). *Seneca: Oxford Readings in Classical Studies*. Oxford; New York, NY. Oxford University Press, 2008.

Shakespeare, William. *Antony & Cleopatra (The Pelican Shakespeare)*, ed. A.R. Braunmuller and Stephen Orgel. New York: Penguin Classics, 1999.

Shakespeare, William. *Shakespeare's Sonnets*, ed. Stephen Booth. New Haven, CT: Yale University Press, 2000.

Siken, Richard. *Crush*. New Haven: Yale University Press, 2005.

Spenser, Edmund. Edmund Spenser's Poetry (NCE), ed. Hugh Maclean and Anne Lake Prescott. New York: W.W. Norton & Co., 1992.

Spicer, Jack (ed. Peter Gizzi). My Vocabulary Did This to Me. Middleton, CT. Wesleyan University Press, 2010.

St. Augustine (trans. R.P.H. Green). *On Christian Doctrine*. New York: Oxford University Press, 1997.

Stein, Gertrude. *Lifting Belly*, ed. Rebecca Mark. Tallahassee, FL: Naiad

Press, 1989.

Virgil (trans. John Dryden). *Aeneid*, ed. Frederick M. Keener. New York: Penguin Classics, 1997.

Winterson, Jeanette. *The Passion*. New York: Grove Press, 1997.

Wordsworth, William. *The Norton Anthology of English Literature, Volume 2: The Romantic Period through the Twentieth Century*, ed. M.H. Abrams et al. New York: W.W. Norton & Co., 2006.

IN THE MUSEUM OF LOST OBJECTS
Pound, Ezra. *The Cantos*. New York: New Directions, 1996.

ON THE SEA employs the Japanese form of the zuihitsu, which translates literally as "following the brush" but more aptly means something like "occasional writings". The best-known examples of zuihitsu can be found in The Pillow Book of Sei Shonagon, an 11th-century text penned over the course of many years by a lady-in-waiting to the empress of Japan.

GREEK EASTER is for Robin Arnold.

VERSUS borrows much of its simple recurring imagery from the paintings of Boyce Cummings, whose work often juxtaposes certain items attended to in great detail with the broader sweep of a background, sometimes even rendered as incomplete. Boyce's art often explores the intimacies of human experiences or relationships without revealing certain kinds of identifying information (such as race). They are a brilliant study in how and where (and to what end) we place our attentions.

OBSESSIONAL is for Jill Alexander Essbaum.

CIRCUS ANIMAL owes its title to W.B. Yeats' "The Circus Animal's Desertion," whose final lines read: "...Now that my ladder's gone /

I must lie down where all the ladders start / In the foul rag and bone shop of the heart."

Status Update is for Michael Morse.

Dispatches from an Unfinished World is for Maurice Manning.

THANKS

Thank you to Dominic Luxford and Jesse Nathan, who believed in me enough to share the immense rational and emotional work of this manuscript, which they did faithfully, meticulously, sincerely, intelligently, cheerfully, and unflaggingly. They are not only my editors, they are my dear friends, my co-conspirators.

Endless thanks also to everyone at McSweeney's who read or proofed or checked facts or otherwise helped this book along: Britta Ameel, Brian McMullen, Walter Green, Adam Krefman, John Babbott, Mackenzie Beer, Charlotte Crowe, Ryan Diaz, Jennifer Florin, Daniel Gumbiner, Victoria Havlicek, Jordan Karnes, Charlotte Locke, Nate Mayer, Anna Noyes, Jessica Tan, Miranda Tsang, Mike Valente, and Libby Wachtler.

Many thanks to Donald Revell, beloved teacher, mentor, friend; and to Craig Dworkin, best of advisors comrades. Thank you to the other members of my brilliant supervisory committee—Vincent Cheng, Karen Brennan, and Margaret Toscano. Thanks also to Mark Strand, Jackie Osherow, Paisley Rekdal, and Marie Ponsot, from whom I have also learned a tremendous amount about writing poems.

To my amazing family—Nancy and Steve Lindenberg, Emily Zuccaro and Tony Zuccaro, thank you so much for your steadfast and good-natured support, for your immense and unwavering generosity. To my other family—Judy and John Arnold, Chris Arnold, and Augusta Palmer, thank you for your acceptance, your love, and your trust.

I owe a profound and enduring debt of gratitude to my friends: Tim O'Keefe, for his unerring sound advice and for always bringing the good beer; Kathryn Cowles and Geoff Babbitt, for their warmth, intelligence, good humor, and exquisite taste in cheese, in whose red chair many of these poems were begun; Jessica Piazza, for always telling me what she thinks; Mandy Brown and Keith "Keef" Ehrlich, Chris Hayes, Danielle Deulan, Dawn Lonsinger, Derek Henderson, Taylor Baldwin, Sara Eliza Johnson, Margaret Reges, Michael Morse, Melissa Tuckey, Matt Bollinger, Greg Schutz, and the others from the University of Utah and the Fine Arts Work Center whose advice and conversation helped inspire, occasion, and refine many, many of these poems. Thank you to Claudia Keelan, especially, and to Forrest Gander and Maurice Manning for their kind and insightful reading of some or all of these poems, and for sharing their poetic know-how.

Thank you to Joseph Bradbury for helping me see this through to the end, and understand it is not the end—for helping me to know that in life and in poems, there is always more to come.

Finally, thank you to Robin Blake Arnold, for being a witty, gentle, and empathic young person and for permitting himself to be dragged all over tarnation in pursuit of the sublime.

And above all to you, Craig Arnold—thank you. Thank you.

ABOUT THE AUTHOR

Rebecca Lindenberg's poems appear in the *Believer*, *POETRY*, *Smartish Pace*, *32 Poems*, *Colorado Review*, *DIAGRAM*, *Denver Quarterly*, and elsewhere. She is the recipient of a literature grant from the National Endowment for the Arts and residencies from the MacDowell Colony and the Provincetown Fine Arts Work Center, and she holds a Ph.D. in Literature and Creative Writing from the University of Utah. Lindenberg lives in northern Utah, where she enjoys a rye Manhattan, a good game of Scrabble, new snow, and her growing menagerie of pets.